INDIAN DESIGNS

FOR JEWELRY AND OTHER ARTS AND CRAFTS

By Connie Asch

Revised

TREASURE CHEST PUBLICATIONS, INC.
P.O. BOX 5250
TUCSON, AZ 85703-0250

NOTE TO THE READER

The designs in this book are primarily for silversmiths, but are adaptable to many other arts and crafts. They may be traced, photo-copied, enlarged, reduced or cut directly from this book.

SYMBOLISM

There have been many inquiries as to the meaning of the designs in this book. The answer is—there are none!

After a design is finished, the person making it will see a resemblance to some natural object and will give it a name. What resembles an arrow point to one person may be a teepee to another.

ACKNOWLEDGEMENTS

I wish to thank the following people
for their help in making this book possible:

O. T. Branson
Nancie Mahan
Sterling Mahan
Cliff Oliver
Jane Oliver

DRAWINGS BY CONNIE ASCH

ISBN-13: 978-0-918080-25-7; ISBN-10: 0-918080-25-8

TREASURE CHEST PUBLICATIONS, INC.
P.O. Box 5250
Tucson, AZ 85703

Printed in Canada

The designs on the next two pages are actual size for use on miniature silver or ceramic pots, as shown in INDIAN JEWELRY MAKING VOL. I, by O. T. Branson. These are adaptable for small bracelets, overlay on rings, earrings or pins. Many of these designs can be used either as negative or positive. The water snakes on page 3, row 2 are correctly shaped for soldering around a small silver pot.

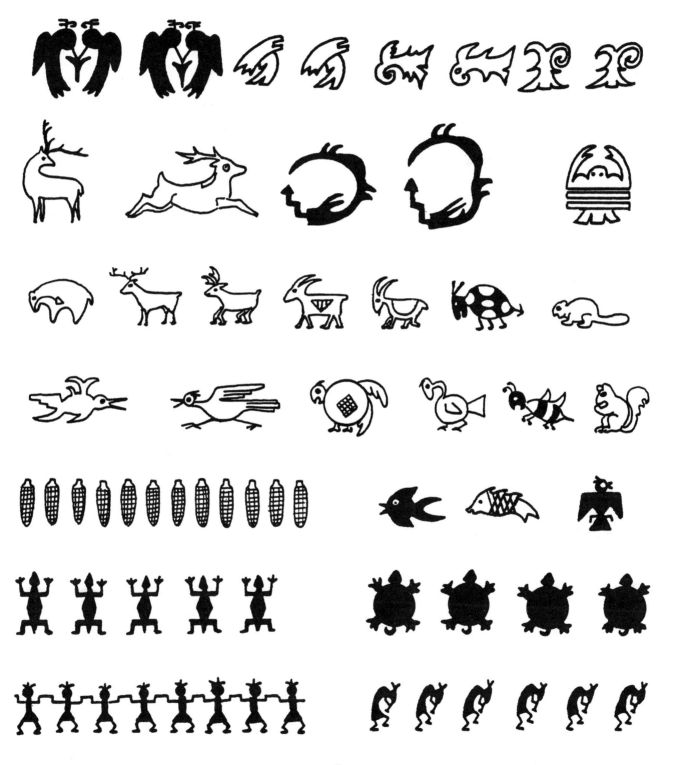

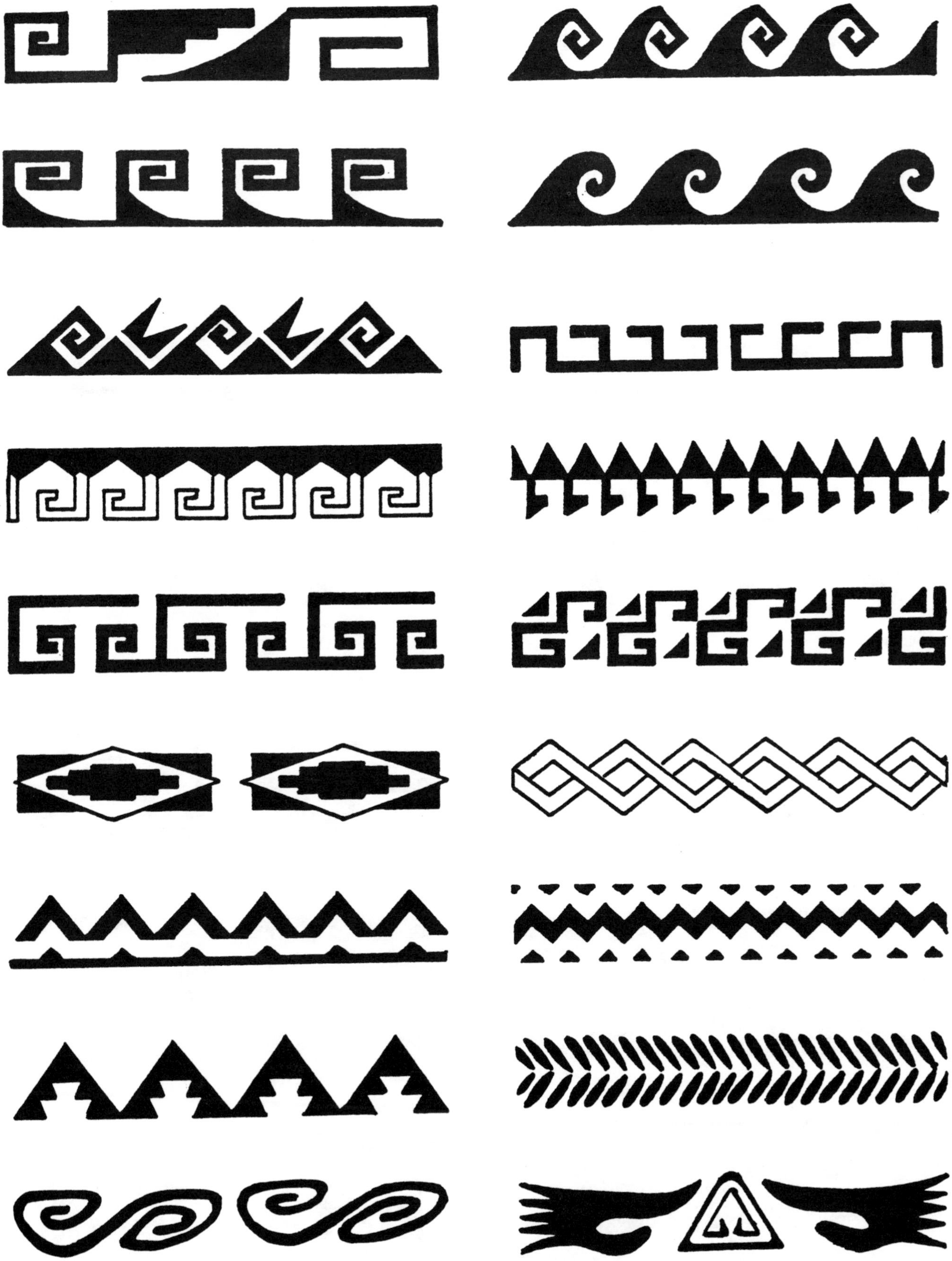

These border designs may be used on baskets, pottery, bracelets, mugs, wind-bells, skirts, shirts or blouses, pillow cases and belts.

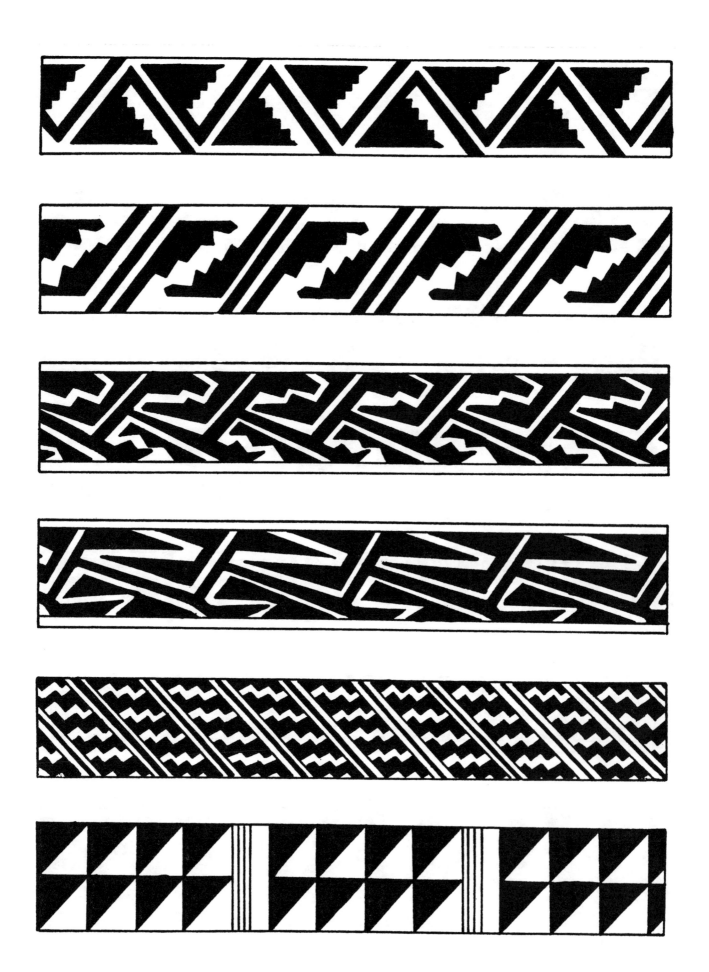

10

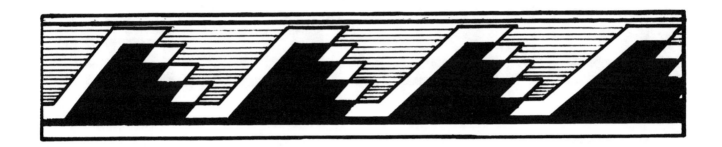

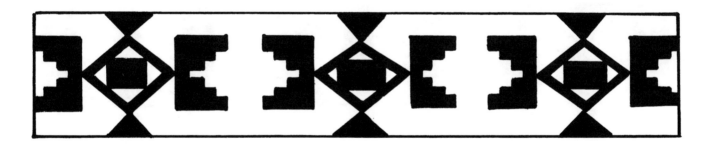

13

Designs on the two bottom rows contract and expand to any length. Combine first and last elements alone or substitute a stone for a center element. To lengthen, repeat center elements. Used alone, the center elements are a complete design.

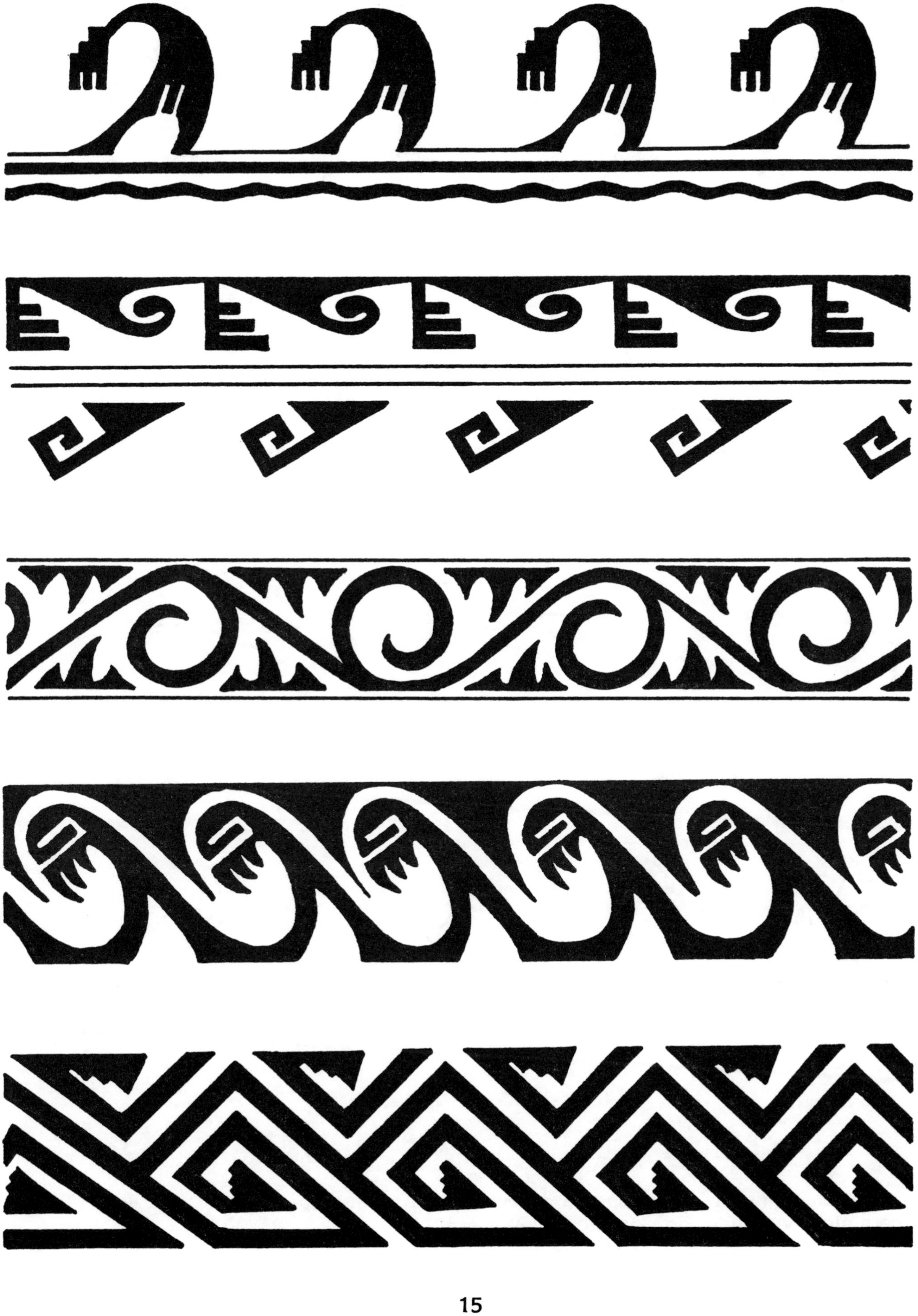

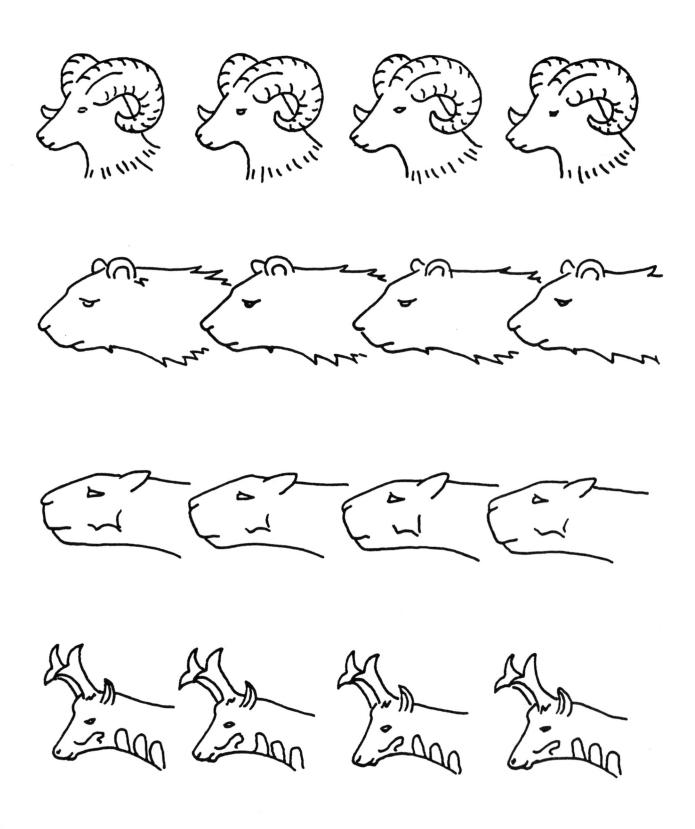

🐢 Use these figures for repousse or overlay on silver cups or bowls, carve on ceramics, embroider on clothing, pillows, etc.

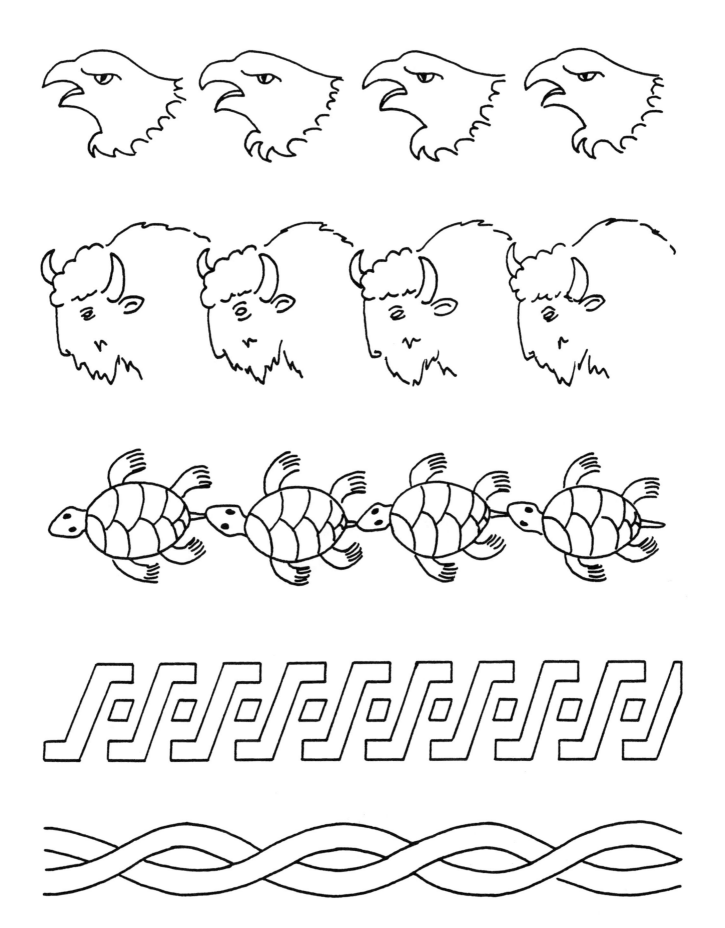

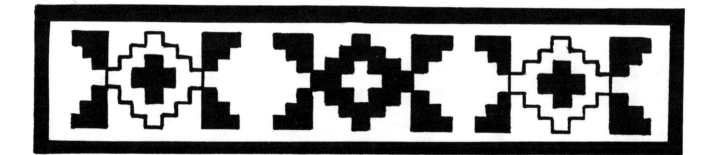

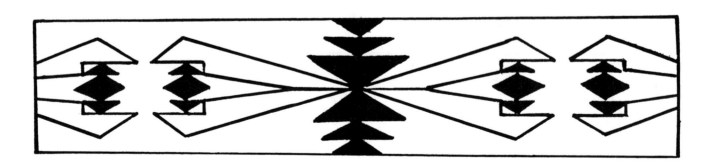

24

A sample of designs for watch bands, bolo ties, pendants, earrings and necklaces. Equally suitable for transfer to leather, fabric or ceramics.

The circular designs on these pages make good pendants, bolo ties, conchos, belt buckles, box tops and bracelets.

Story buckles and bracelets are less complicated than they look. A jeweler's saw, simple liner and small dot punch or stamp are all that is needed for this metalworking. Elements from any of the designs on pages 31 through 33 can be arranged to make up your own story. These are actual size for a bracelet, but may be enlarged for embroidery, leatherwork, wood carvings, pottery, ceramics or other crafts.

31

These are bear paws and hands for bracelets, pendants, pins, buckles, necklaces, bolo ties, small conchos or tie tacks.

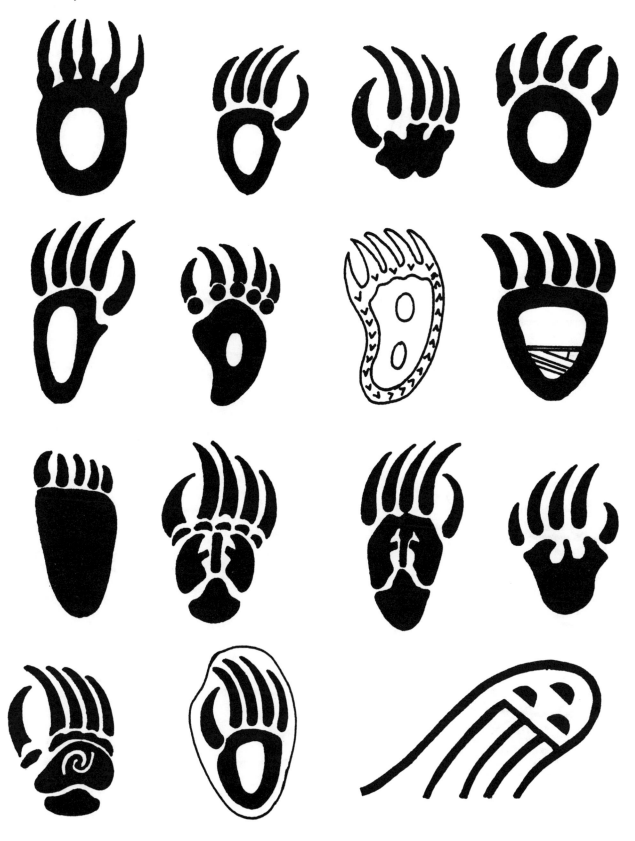

Water snakes for pottery, weaving, embroidery, leather belts and belt buckles, may be used singly or in a series.

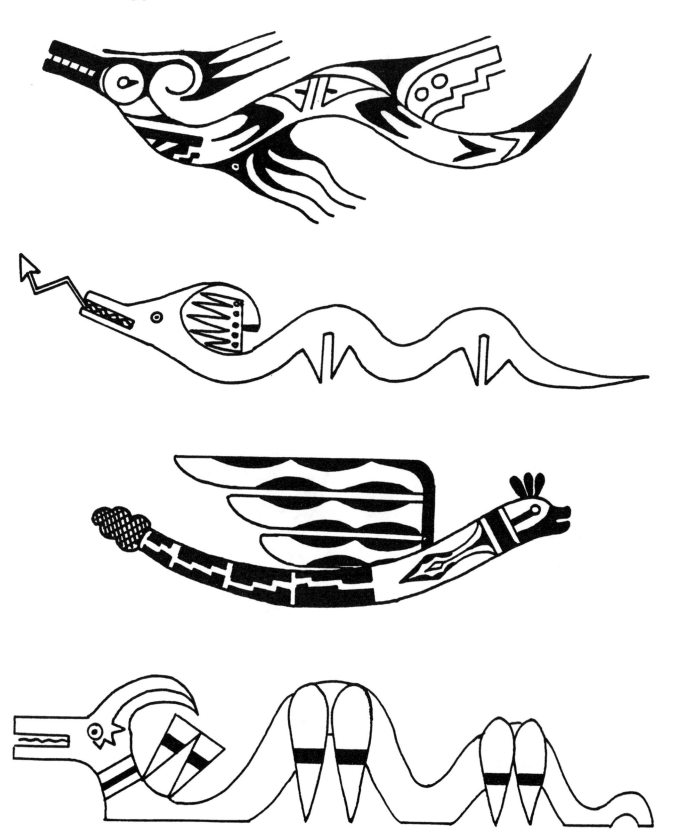

Bird designs may be used as pendants, pins, buckles or bolo ties. They transfer well for pottery, ceramics, wind-bells or mobiles.

 Some of these animal figures are suitable for either flat or three dimensional pieces.

54

These border designs may be used on baskets, pottery, bracelets, mugs, windbells, skirts or blouses, pillow cases or belts, etc.

59

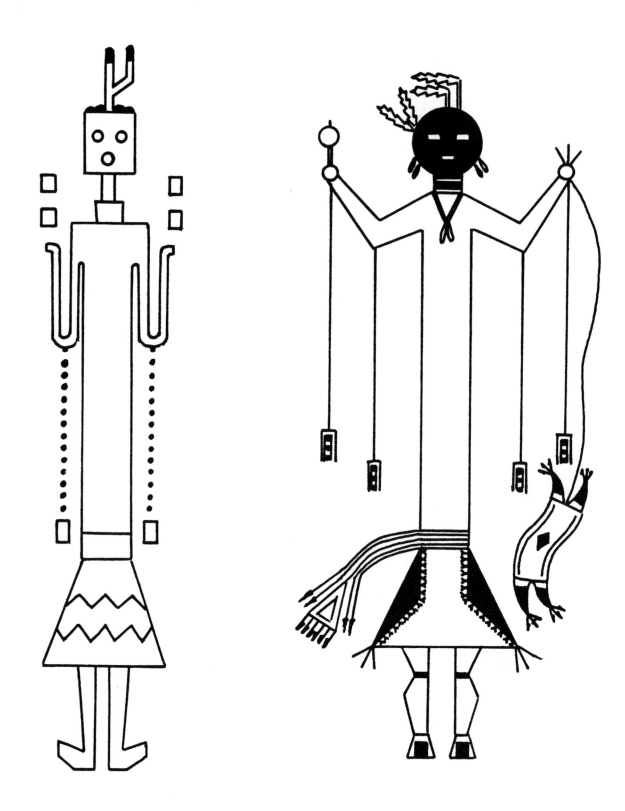

These yei figures make nice designs on large wind-bells, mugs, embroidered borders on long skirts or in small size on pockets, shirt backs or vests.

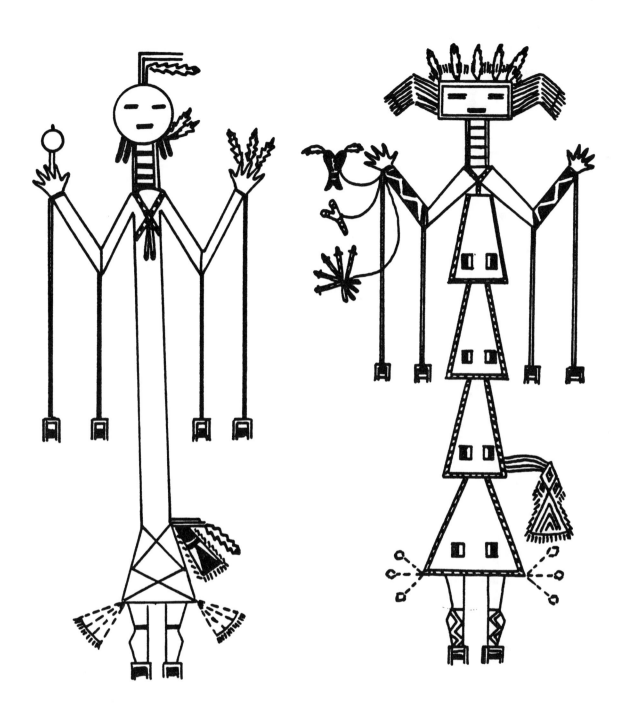

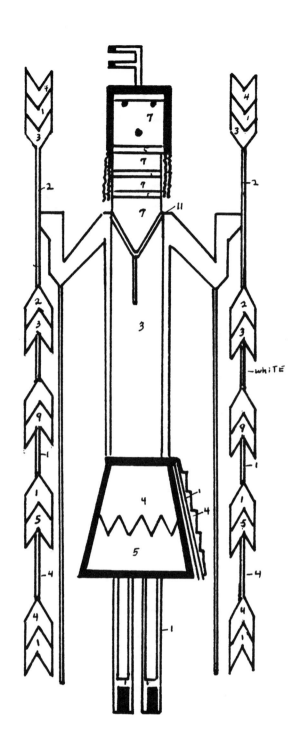
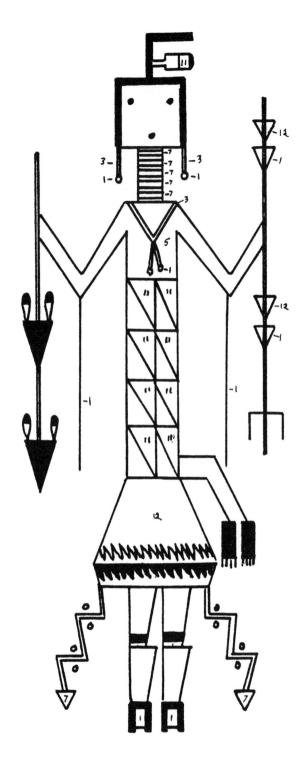

1. RED
2. BLACK
3. BLUE
4. GREEN
5. YELLOW
6. PINK
7. BROWN
8. ORANGE
9. PURPLE
10. DARK BLUE
11. TAN
12. GREY

BIBLIOGRAPHY

ARIZONA HIGHWAYS MAGAZINE, Phoenix, Arizona
    February 1950, Vol. 26, No. 2.
    May 1974, Vol. 50, No. 5.
    July 1974, Vol. 50, No. 7.
    August 1974, Vol. 50, No. 8.
    August 1976, Vol. 52, No. 8.

BENNETT, NOEL, and BIGHORSE, TIANA.
    1971, *Working with the Wool*
    Northland Press, Flagstaff, Arizona

BRANSON, O. T.
    1977, *Indian Jewelry Making*, Vol. I.
    1979, *Indian Jewelry Making*, Vol. II.
    Treasure Chest Publications, Tucson, Arizona

BRODY, J. J.
    1977, *Mimbres Painted Pottery*
    School of American Research, Santa Fe, New Mexico
    University of New Mexico Press, Albuquerque, New Mexico

FERG, ALAN; Editor
    1987, *Western Apache Material Culture, The Goodwin and Guenter Collection*
    University of Arizona Press, Tucson, Arizona

JAMES, GEORGE WARTON
    1974, *Indian Blankets and their Makers*
    Rio Grande Press, Glorieta, New Mexico

JONES, JOAN MEGAN
    1982, *The Art and Style of Western Indian Basketry*
    Hancock House, Blain, Washington

LISTER, ROBERT H. and FLORENCE C.
    1987, *Anasazi Pottery*
    Maxwell Museum of Anthropology and the University of New Mexico Press,
    Albuquerque, New Mexico

KING, DALE STUART
    1976, *Indian Silver*, Vol. II
    Dale Stuart King Publications, Tucson, Arizona

LYFORD, CONNIE A.
    1979, *Quill and Beadwork of the Western Sioux*
    Johnson Publishing Co., Boulder, Colorado

MAXWELL, GILBERT S.
1963, *Navajo Rugs, Past, Present and Future*
Desert Southwest Inc., Palm Desert, California

MAXWELL MUSEUM OF ANTHROPOLOGY
1974, *Seven Families in Pueblo Pottery*
University of New Mexico Press, Albuquerque, New Mexico

NAYLOR, MANIA; Editor
1975, *Authentic Indian Designs*
Dover Publications, Inc., New York, New York

NORDENSKIOLD, GUSTAF N.
1979, *Cliffdwellers of Mesa Verde*
Rio Grande Press, Glorieta, New Mexico

ORCHARD, WILLIAM C.
1971, *The Techniques of Porcupine Quill Decorations Among the Indians of North America*
Eagles View Publishing, Ogden, Utah

ROHN, ARTHUR H.
1971, *Mug House, Mesa Verde National Park, Wetherill Mesa Excavations*
Archeological Research Series Number Seven-D
National Park Service, U.S. Department of Interior, Washington, D.C.

WESHE, ALICE
1977, *Wild Brothers of the Indians*
Treasure Chest Publications, Tucson, Arizona